Food

PASTA

Jillian Powell

WAYLAND

Titles in the series

BREAD EGGS FISH FRUIT MILK
PASTA POTATOES RICE

First published in 1996 by Wayland (Publishers) Ltd
61 Western Road, Hove, East Sussex, BN3 1JD, England

© 1996 Wayland (Publishers) Ltd

Series Editor: Francesca Motisi
Editor: Liz Harman
Designer: Jean Wheeler
Illustrations: Peter Bull
Cover: APM Studios – photostylist Zoë Hargreaves

British Library Cataloguing in Publication Data
Powell, Jillian
Pasta. – (Food)
1. Pasta products – Juvenile literature 2. Cookery (Pasta) – Juvenile literature
I. Title II. Series
41.3'311

ISBN 0 7502 1794 4

Typeset by Jean Wheeler

Printed and bound in Italy by L.E.G.O. S.p.A., Vicenza, Italy

Picture acknowledgements

Allsport 10; Cephas 8, 20, 25; Chapel Studios 9 (top), 11 (top), 12, 13 (bottom), 14, 15 (both), 16, 17 (both), 19 (top), 21 (top), 22–3, 24 (both); Mary Evans 7 (both); Eye Ubiquitous 4, 9 (bottom), 18, 21 (bottom); Life File 13 (top), 19 (bottom); Pasta Information Service 5; Wayland Picture Library title page, contents page, 6, 11 (bottom).

Contents

The healthy fast food 4
Pasta in the past 6
Pasta today 8
The food in pasta 10
The pasta factory 12
Making pasta 14
Cooking pasta 16
Italy – home of pasta 18
Italian pasta dishes 20
An A to Z of pasta shapes 22
Pasta dishes from around the world 24
Pasta recipes for you to try 26
Glossary 30
Books to read 31
Index 32

The healthy fast food

Pasta is eaten by millions of people around the world. Many countries have pasta shops, restaurants and take-aways. In Italy, which is thought of as the home of pasta, every region has its own kinds of pasta and special pasta recipes. In China and Japan, a type of pasta called noodles is very popular. Noodles are sold by street sellers, eaten in restaurants and cooked at home in every kind of dish from soups to stir frys.

Pasta is an Italian word meaning a paste or dough made from wheat flour, water and sometimes eggs. Dough for bread is baked in an oven, but pasta or noodle dough is rolled out flat, then cut into shapes and boiled in water.

◀ This Chinese boy is using chopsticks to eat a bowl of noodles.

Pasta comes in hundreds of different shapes, including ribbons, tubes, stars, shells, spirals, bows and even cartoon characters and alphabet letters. Pasta can also be different colours.

Pasta is a fast food because it is quick and easy to cook. There are lots of ways to eat pasta: hot or cold, in soups, salads and with vegetable, meat or sweet sauces.

Pasta is an energy-giving food that is good for you, especially if you eat it with healthy, low-fat foods like vegetable sauces and salads.

▲ Pasta is a healthy, energy-giving food and contains no additives (like artificial colours or flavours).

In Italy, the home of pasta, every person eats an average of 26 kilograms of pasta each year.

Pasta in the past

People have been eating pasta for about 7,000 years. No one knows who invented pasta but we do know that it was eaten in ancient Egypt, China and Japan and by the ancient Greeks and Romans. There are ancient wall paintings in Italy that show cooks making lasagne, and thin sticks found in Etruscan tombs may have been used for winding dough into macaroni. A recipe for strips of pasta fried with pepper and honey appears in one of the earliest recipe books, which was written by the Roman cook Apicius in the first century AD.

▼ Freshly made Chinese noodles hanging up to dry in the sun. Noodles have been made like this in China for centuries.

Pasta was a popular food in the Middle Ages. Italian household accounts show that people bought macaroni and lasagne as well as special slotted spoons used for draining pasta. The thirteenth-century Italian explorer Marco Polo wrote that 'Chinese noodles taste very good and similar to certain lasagne which we eat.'

Pasta was first made in factories during the nineteenth century in southern Italy, where the warm winds were ideal for drying the sheets of pasta. It was said that pasta makers knew more about the weather than sailors, because they knew exactly when the wind changed direction.

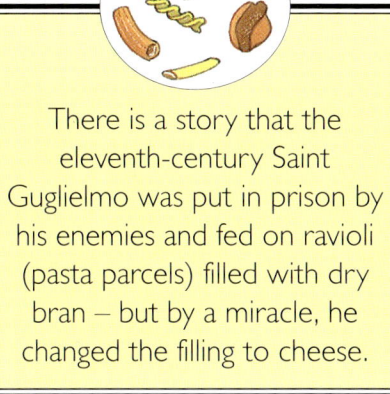

There is a story that the eleventh-century Saint Guglielmo was put in prison by his enemies and fed on ravioli (pasta parcels) filled with dry bran – but by a miracle, he changed the filling to cheese.

◀ An Italian pasta advertisement from 1940.

▶ Macaronis were fashionable young men in eighteenth-century London.

Italian cooks spread the taste for pasta around the world. In 1789, Thomas Jefferson, who later became President of the USA, sent for a 'machine for macaroni' from Naples, Italy. In Britain, during the eighteenth century, rich young men went on grand tours of Italy to study art and culture. This led to a fashion for everything Italian, including pasta. In London, there was a club whose members were called the Macaronis because they had fallen in love with Italy and pasta, especially macaroni. They even wrote poems in praise of pasta.

Pasta today

Today, pasta can be bought in lots of different forms – fresh, dried, frozen or canned. Most of the pasta we eat is made from durum wheat flour. Durum wheat produces a hard grain, which is ground into a rough, yellow flour called semola. This is mixed with water and sometimes eggs to make pasta dough. The dough is rolled out into thin sheets and put in to moulds or cut into different shapes.

Fresh pasta is still made in many Italian homes. It can be made with a finely ground wheat flour called semolina, or from buckwheat or wheat flour, like that used to make bread, mixed with eggs. Italian cooks are skilled at kneading and rolling the dough out thinly before cutting it with knives or putting it through hand machines to make the different shapes.

Fresh pasta can be bought in delicatessens and supermarkets as well as restaurants and take-aways. It takes only two or three minutes to cook in boiling water. It does not stay fresh and must be used in a day or two.

▼ Pasta can be made into lots of different shapes by hand or by machine.

Most of the pasta we buy today has been dried, which means that it can be kept for several months. When it is cooked in boiling water the dry, hard shapes absorb water, soften and puff up. Dried pasta doubles in size and weight when it is cooked.

Noodles can be made from wheat or rice flour or ground mung beans. Sometimes egg is added to make egg noodles. Like pasta, noodles are also sold fresh or dried. Chinese noodle makers are very skilled and take four or five years to learn their craft. They knead, pull, toss and twist the dough to make long, fine noodles. Dried noodles are soaked in water to soften them before cooking and they take longer to cook than fresh noodles.

▲ Noodles can be many different sizes and colours.

▼ A skilled Chinese noodle maker at work.

The food in pasta

Pasta is good for you. It contains lots of carbohydrates, which give you energy. Food energy is measured in kilocalories. Other healthy foods such as bread, rice and potatoes also contain lots of carbohydrates. High carbohydrate foods are an important part of a healthy diet. Pasta is a filling food and contains half the kilocalories of meat. Pasta is special because it releases energy more slowly than other foods.

▶ Athletes taking part in marathon races or tiring sports often eat pasta the night before an event because it releases energy slowly.

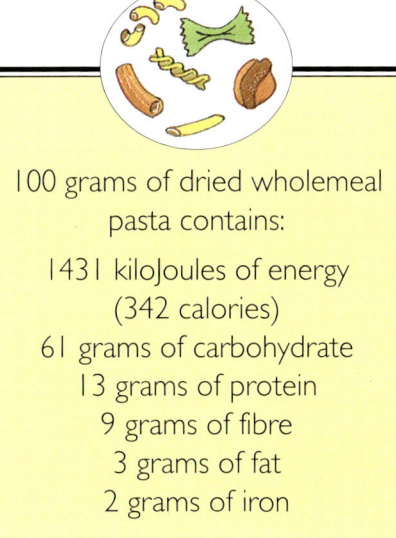

100 grams of dried wholemeal pasta contains:

1431 kiloJoules of energy (342 calories)
61 grams of carbohydrate
13 grams of protein
9 grams of fibre
3 grams of fat
2 grams of iron

◀ Wholewheat pasta (left) contains twice as much fibre as refined 'white' pasta (right).

Pasta contains fibre, which is sometimes called roughage. Fibre helps us to digest food and pass it through our bodies. Wholewheat pasta is twice as good for you because it contains over twice as much fibre as pasta made with flour which has been milled to remove the bran.

Pasta contains protein, which is needed to build up the body and keep it healthy. Pasta has more protein than potatoes or rice and almost as much as beef, so it is good for vegetarians – people who choose not to eat meat. Pasta also gives us some of the vitamins and minerals that we need to help our bodies to work properly. For example, pasta contains the mineral iron, which keeps the blood healthy.

Pasta is low in fat, which is good because too much fat can damage the heart. It contains no added sugar or salt, which is good because sugar can harm the teeth and too much salt is bad for the heart.

▲ Pasta is easy to cook and makes a filling and healthy meal.

The pasta factory

Pasta and noodles are made from wheat, the world's most widely grown cereal crop. The starchy grain is ground to make flour. At the pasta factory, the flour is mixed with water to make a paste. Eggs are added for egg noodles and for certain types of pasta like tagliatelle (see page 22) and for pasta that will be sold fresh, for cooking straight away.

▼ Pasta is made from wheat flour, ground from grains of wheat like these.

Pasta dough is pressed into moulds or pushed through machines that cut out the different pasta shapes – strands, tubes, spirals, shells and hundreds of other varieties. Some kinds of pasta, like ravioli and tortellini, are folded and filled with meat, cheese or vegetables.

◀ Pasta can be different colours because some ingredients add colour. Wholemeal flour makes brown pasta, tomato or beetroot juice makes red pasta and spinach juice makes green pasta.

▼ Pasta numbers in tomato sauce is a popular children's dish, usually sold in cans.

Some factory-made pasta is made into ready-to-eat pasta dishes like macaroni cheese or spaghetti bolognaise, which are chilled or frozen and just need to be re-heated. Dishes such as ravioli (meat-filled pasta parcels), spaghetti shapes in tomato sauce or minestrone soup can also be sold in tin cans, which keep fresh for a long time.

Pasta may also be dried, so that it will keep fresh in bags or boxes for several months. Pasta takes between forty and eighty hours to dry, depending on its shape.

Finally, the pasta is packaged and sent to shops to be sold.

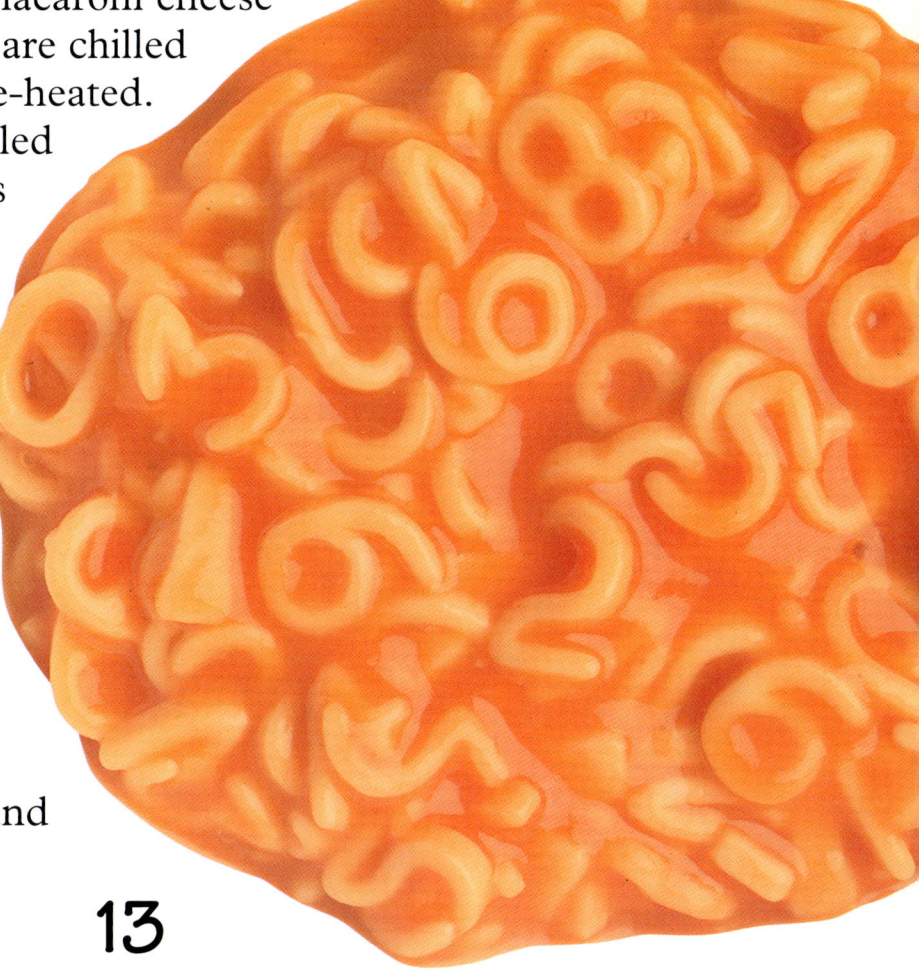

Making pasta

Making pasta is very easy. Fresh pasta can be made in the kitchen at home with just a few simple ingredients.

To make fresh egg pasta, you will need:

1 medium egg
100 g strong, unbleached plain flour.

Carefully pour the flour into a heap on a big pastry board and use your hands to make a hole in the middle. Break the egg into the hole and use your hands to work the egg into the flour (this is called 'kneading') until it sticks together and feels damp and stretchy. Don't let the dough dry out or it will be difficult to work with. If it starts to feel dry you can add a few drops of water. Now wrap the dough in a damp cloth and put it in the refrigerator.

◀ This boy is kneading fresh pasta dough.

After fifteen minutes, take out the ball of dough and use your hands to press it out into a circle on a floured board. Then use a rolling pin and, working from the middle outwards, begin rolling out the dough. When you have a sheet of dough, turn it over, and roll it out again until it is thin and even.

Sprinkle it with flour, then leave it to dry for about thirty minutes before cutting out your pasta shapes. One way of making thin strips is to fold the sheet several times and then cut thin slices.

Your fresh egg pasta will take only two or three minutes to cook in boiling water.

▲ Using a rolling pin to make a thin, flat sheet of pasta. Dust the rolling pin with flour to stop it sticking.

◀ Cutting out pasta shapes by hand.

Cooking pasta

Allow about 75 g of pasta for each person. You will need a large pan, about three-quarters full of water. Allow about 1–1½ litres of water for every 100 grams of pasta.

Cover the pan and ask an adult to help you to put it on the cooker and bring the water to the boil. Add a pinch of salt, then add the pasta and stir with a wooden spoon. Bring the water back to the boil then turn down the heat so that the water is bubbling fast but will not boil over.

If you are cooking fresh pasta, it will only take two or three minutes to cook. Dried pasta will take longer to cook – probably 10 to 20 minutes. You will find cooking times on the packet.

▼ Pasta cooks quickly in boiling water.

▶ Testing to see if the pasta is cooked.

When you think the pasta is ready, use a spoon or fork and carefully remove a piece of pasta from the water. Let it cool slightly and then taste it to see if it ready. Pasta should be slightly chewy – not too hard, but not too soft or mushy either. The Italians call this cooking *al dente*, which means 'to the tooth'. You may have to leave the pasta to boil for a bit longer, then test it again.

When your pasta is ready, ask an adult to help you take the pan off the heat and drain the pasta. You can stir in a few drops of olive oil or a little butter, which can help to prevent the pasta from sticking together.

◀ Adding a little olive oil to cooked pasta.

Italy – home of pasta

Italy is the home of pasta. Italians have been eating pasta for thousands of years and every region has different kinds of pasta and many ways of cooking it. There are pasta shops that sell loose pasta, and many Italians still make fresh pasta at home. They eat it as a starter, main or sweet course, sometimes twice a day.

▼ Lasagne is a popular Italian dish of pasta, meat, vegetables and sauce that is eaten all over the world.

Special pasta dishes are eaten at Christmas time. Cappelletti ('little hats') are served at Christmas and New Year, when they may be filled with left-over Christmas turkey. Passatelli is a pasta soup with cheese that is served in Bologna at Easter and during the spring. Pasta is also a popular festival food. In Naples, baskets of hot pasta pies called pasticci and timballi are sold by street sellers on festival days.

▶ Ravioli served with a tomato sauce.

In Italy, it is important to choose the right sauce for the right pasta. Fine strands of pasta are usually served with a light sauce, but short, stubby shapes will have a chunkier sauce. In sweet dishes, pasta may be served with a dressing of ricotta cheese, sugar and cinnamon, or filled with dried or candied fruits. In the Umbria region, there is even a chocolate cake made from pasta.

▶ Yellow and green pasta mixed together are called 'straw and hay' in Italy. There is a Roman saying that means 'Be they hay or be they straw, fill the stomach with pasta galore!'.

Italian pasta dishes

Pasta is eaten all over Italy and different dishes are popular in each region of the country.

▲ Linguine – a favourite dish in the South.

Cooks in Liguria add chopped herbs to their pasta dough. The pasta is served with pesto, a sauce made from basil, pine nuts, olive oil and parmesan, a hard cheese.

Fettuccine, a type of noodle popular in Rome, is said to be the width of a dressmaker's tape and as straight as a Roman road. Also from Rome comes spaghetti carbonara, a dish that took its name from the charcoal burners in the woods who traditionally made this dish using spaghetti, bacon, eggs and cheese.

In parts of southern Italy, pasta is often served with seafood or hot sauces made with chillie peppers.

Cooks in Abruzzi make a dish called *maccheroni alla chitarra*. The name comes from the machine used to make the pasta, which looks like a guitar. Egg pasta is rolled into flat sheets then pushed through wires on a wooden frame. It is served with hot chillie sauce in locally-made pottery bowls.

Pasta is especially popular in Sicily. It was once said that every Sicilian dreamed of a Sicily made out of macaroni, with Mount Etna (a volcano in Sicily) as a mountain of grated cheese and the lighthouse in the harbour full of wine.

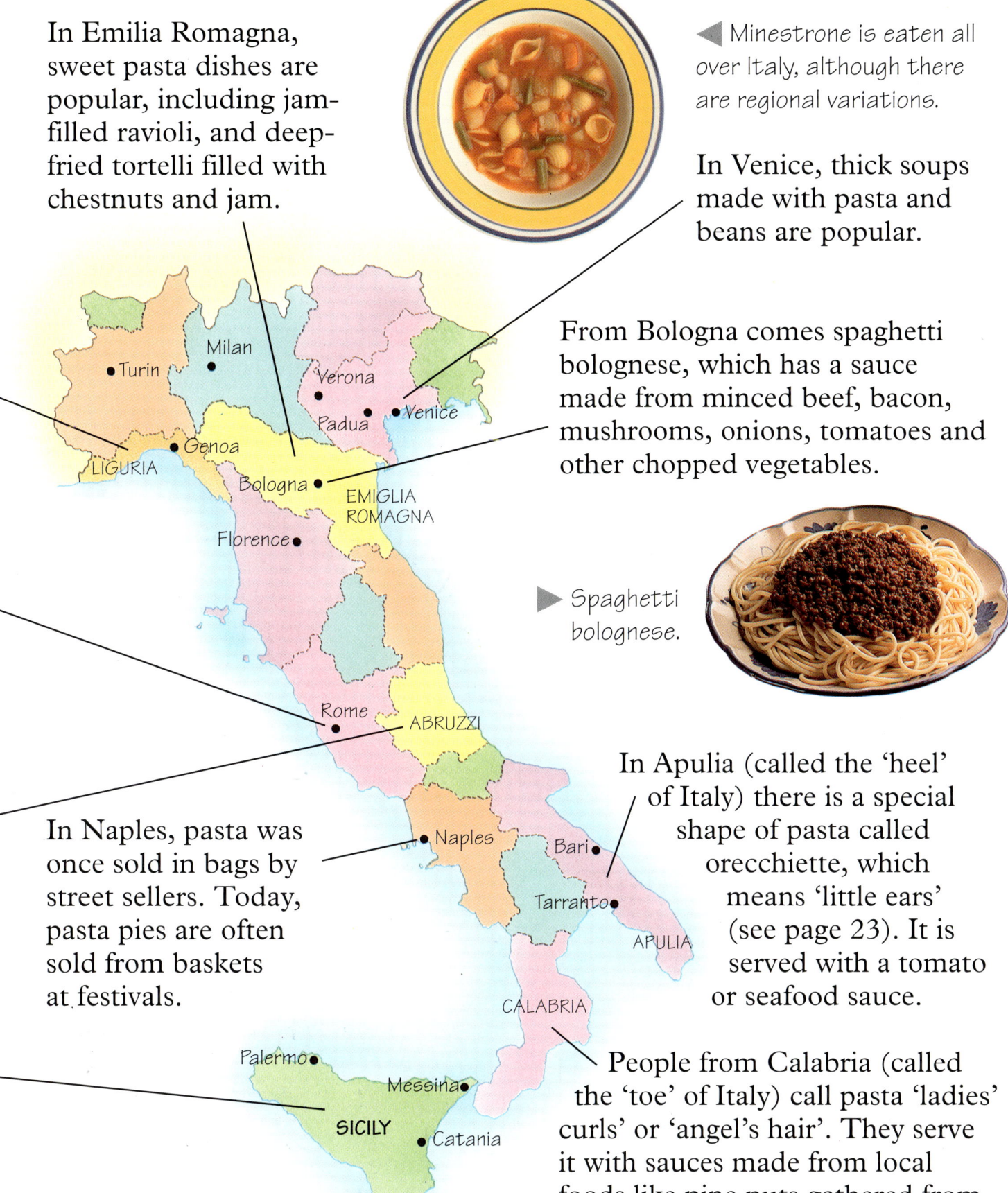

In Emilia Romagna, sweet pasta dishes are popular, including jam-filled ravioli, and deep-fried tortelli filled with chestnuts and jam.

◀ Minestrone is eaten all over Italy, although there are regional variations.

In Venice, thick soups made with pasta and beans are popular.

From Bologna comes spaghetti bolognese, which has a sauce made from minced beef, bacon, mushrooms, onions, tomatoes and other chopped vegetables.

▶ Spaghetti bolognese.

In Naples, pasta was once sold in bags by street sellers. Today, pasta pies are often sold from baskets at festivals.

In Apulia (called the 'heel' of Italy) there is a special shape of pasta called orecchiette, which means 'little ears' (see page 23). It is served with a tomato or seafood sauce.

People from Calabria (called the 'toe' of Italy) call pasta 'ladies' curls' or 'angel's hair'. They serve it with sauces made from local foods like pine nuts gathered from the woods, and spicy sausages.

An A to Z of pasta shapes

There are about 600 kinds of pasta and new ones are being invented all the time. Pasta comes in flat sheets, like lasagne, tubes like macaroni and cannelloni, strings like spaghetti, and 'nests' like vermicelli and tagliatelle. There are also spirals, shells, rings and bows.

In Italy, each region makes its own traditional shapes and they all have nicknames. For example, tortellini are known as the tummy button of Venus, the Roman goddess of love. Italian cooks know which sauces to use with each kind of pasta.

> Tagliatelle was said to have been created in 1487 in honour of the long, blonde hair of Lucrezia Borgia, a famous Italian noblewoman of the time. For centuries, Italian cooks argued over how wide tagliatelle should be. In 1972 it was decided that tagliatelle should be 8 mm wide when cooked; anything else was not tagliatelle.

▶ A selection of various pasta shapes.

22

Key

1. Elbow rigatoni
2. Fusilli
3. Cannelloni
4. Conchiglie rigate
5. Spaghetti
6. Cappelletti
7. Orecchiette
8. Tagliatelle
9. Farfalle
10. Gemelli
11. Pappardelle
12. Lumache
13. Rigatoni
14. Penne
15. Lasagne
16. Conchiglie

anelli	rings
bucatini	long tubes
cannelloni	large tubes
cappelletti	'little hats'
conchiglie	shells
farfalle	bows or butterflies
fettuccine	nests of wide strands
fusilli	corkscrews
gemelli	twins – two strands twisted together
lasagne	flat sheets
lumache	large 'snails'
macaroni	short tubes
orecchiette	'little ears'
pappardelle	nests of wide strips
penne	pens (because they look like old-fashioned quill pens)
ravioli	stuffed squares
riccie	curly noodles
rigatoni	ridged tubes
spaghetti	strings
stelline	'little stars'
tagliatelle	nests of strands
tortellini	round twists of stuffed pasta
tortiglioni	twists
vermicelli	'little worms'
ziti	long macaroni

Pasta dishes from around the world

Pasta is eaten in many different ways around the world. In parts of Germany and eastern France, cooks make a special pasta called spätzle from flour, eggs and cream. The fine strands are poached in boiling water then served with meat or cheese sauce.

▶ Creamy German spätzle, served with cheese sauce.

▼ A Chinese dish of noodles and vegetables.

Sometimes pasta is filled or stuffed, in dishes such as Chinese won ton, Russian pel'meni, Tibetan molmo and Jewish kreplachs.

In China, Japan and other eastern countries, noodles are popular and are eaten at all times of day from breakfast to dinner. They are boiled and eaten in soups and sauces, fried and served with meat and vegetables, or eaten cold in salads.

Noodles come in all shapes and sizes (see page 9). Flat noodles are usually used in soups, and rounded noodles in stir-fry dishes. Noodles can be made from wheat or rice flour. Rice noodles are popular in southern China, eaten with seafood. Bean thread or cellophane noodles are made from ground mung beans and are very fine strands that are almost see-through. Cooks deep fry them to serve with meat or vegetable dishes, or put them in soups and casseroles.

Egg noodles, which are made by adding egg to the pasta dough, are served with lots of different sauces, which can be made with fish, meat, chicken or vegetables. For a simple stir fry, noodles may be fried with some bean sprouts and spring onions in a little sesame oil, rice wine and soy sauce.

Noodles are often served on birthdays in China and are traditionally eaten at New Year, because the long strands represent long life. It is thought to be unlucky to cut them, as this might shorten your life.

▼ Noodles being cooked outdoors on a market stall in China.

Pasta recipes for you to try

Chow mein

For this stir-fry dish, a Chinese wok is best but you could use a large frying pan.

To serve four people you will need:

225 g fresh or dried egg noodles
25 g smoked bacon, chopped finely
1 tablespoon chopped spring onions
50 g peas
1 teaspoon light soy sauce

1 tablespoon oil
1 chopped garlic clove
$\frac{1}{2}$ teaspoon sugar
1 teaspoon sesame oil

1 Cook the noodles, following the instructions on the packet. Dried noodles will take a few minutes longer to cook than fresh noodles. Put the noodles in cold water to cool until you are ready to use them.

2 Ask an adult to help you to heat a tablespoon of oil in the wok or frying pan, and fry the garlic for about ten seconds.

3 Add the peas and the bacon, and keep stirring as you fry them for another minute.

4 Drain the noodles in a sieve and put them into the pan with the soy sauce, sugar and spring onions. Cook, stirring well, for another two to four minutes.

5 Add the sesame oil, stir again, then turn out your chow mein on to a hot serving dish.

27

Sweet rigatoni

Try this sweet pasta as an unusual sweet course.

To serve four people you will need:

200 g of rigatoni or another short kind of pasta
100 g ricotta cheese
2 rounded teaspoons caster sugar
¼ teaspoon powdered cinnamon
about 60–75 ml milk

1 Ask an adult to help you heat a pan of water until it is boiling.

2 Add a pinch of salt to the boiling water, then carefully add the pasta. Stir with a wooden spoon and cook for the length of time stated on the packet.

3 Pour the milk into a small saucepan and heat gently until it is just warm.

4 In a bowl, mix together the ricotta cheese, sugar and cinnamon. Gradually mix in a little of the warm milk until the sauce is creamy but not too runny.

5 Ask an adult to help you to drain the cooked pasta, then mix it with the ricotta sauce and turn it in to a warm serving dish.

29

Glossary

bran The coating of a cereal grain such as rice or wheat, between the outer hull and the inner seed.

carbohydrate Foods including sugars and starches, which give us energy.

cereal A kind of plant that produces grain.

charcoal burners People who burn wood very slowly, to make charcoal.

delicatessens Shops or parts of shops that sell fresh foods.

dough A paste of flour and water.

dressing A sauce that is put on to food.

Etruscan Belonging to an ancient people who lived in central Italy before the Romans.

fibre A part of food that helps the body digest and pass food through.

grand tour A trip taken by rich eighteenth-century men to study the art and literature of Europe.

kilocalories Measurements of the energy in food.

kneading Working and shaping with the hands.

marathon A long race.

Middle Ages The time in history from the fifth to the fifteenth century.

milled Ground up. Seeds and cereal grains are often milled.

minerals Substances found in food that we need to keep our bodies healthy.

mung beans A kind of bean grown in Asia.

poached Cooked in boiling liquid or steam.

protein A substance found in food that we need to grow and repair our bodies.

roughage A substance found in food, that helps our bodies to digest and pass food through.

starch A type of carbohydrate.

stir fry A method of cooking by frying food quickly in oil, stirring it all the time.

vegetarians People who choose not to eat meat.

vitamins Substances found in food that we need to keep us healthy.

wholemeal and **wholewheat** The whole grain including the outer husk or bran.

wok A rounded Chinese pan used for frying food.

Books to read

Pasta by Kate Haycock (Wayland, 1990)

A Taste of China by Roz Denny (Wayland, 1994)

A Taste of Italy by Jenny Ridgewell (Wayland, 1993)

A Taste of Japan by Jenny Ridgewell (Wayland, 1993)

For further information about pasta, contact:
The Pasta Information Centre
26 Fitzroy Square
London W1P 6BT
Tel. 0171 388 7421

Index

Numbers in **bold** show subjects that appear in pictures.

ancient Greeks 6
ancient Romans 6
anelli 23
Apicius (Roman cook) 6
athletes **10**

Borgia, Lucrezia 22
bran 11
bucatini 23

canned pasta 8, 13
cannelloni **22**, 22, 23
cappelletti 18, **22**, 23
carbohydrates 10
China 4, **6**, 6, **9**, 24, **25**, 25
chow mein 26–7
Christmas 18
conchiglie **22**, 23
cooking pasta 16–17

Easter 18
Egypt 6

factories 7, 12, 13
farfalle **22**, 23
fettuccine 20, 23
fibre 11
France 24
fusilli **22**, 23

gemelli **23**, 23
Germany 24

grand tour 7
Guglielmo, Saint 7
Italy 4, 5, 6, 7, 18–19, 20–21, 22
Japan 4, 6, 24
Jefferson, Thomas 7

kilocalories 10

lasagne 6, **18**, 22, **23**, 23
linguine **20**
lumache **23**, 23

macaroni 6, 7, 13, 20, 22, 23
Macaronis 7, 7
making pasta 8–9, 12–13, 14–15
Middle Ages 6
minerals 11
minestrone 13, **21**
Mount Etna 20

New Year 18, 25
noodles **4**, 4, **6**, 6, **9**, 9, **24**, 24, **25**, 25

orecchiette 21, **22**, 23

pappardelle **23**, 23
parmesan 20
passatelli 18
pasticci 18
penne **23**, 23
pesto 21

Polo, Marco 6
protein 11

ravioli 7, 12, **13**, **19**, 20, 23
riccie 23
rigatoni **23**, 23

semola 8
semolina 8
Sicily 20
spaghetti 13, 20, 21, **22**, 22, 23
spaghetti bolognese 13, **21**, 21
spaghetti carbonara 20
spätzle **24**, 24
stelline 23

tagliatelle 12, **22**, 22, 23
timballi 18
tortelli 20
tortellini 12, 22, 23
tortiglioni 23

USA 7

vermicelli 22, 23
vitamins 11

wheat 4, 8, **12**, 12, 13
wholewheat pasta **11**, 11

ziti 23

32